she never leaves home without: her iPhone
the best advice she ever received: don't believe the hype!
she is totally addicted to: lipgloss
her superpower wish is to: take over the world!
the person she texts most is: her mom and Selena

demi hates: rumours
favourite food: Demi would choose tacos over pizza
first concert: Santana
language she is learning: French
weird food confession: Demi loves pickles, cheese, eggs, homemade Rice Krispy treats, and chocolate
she loves: poetry

she was starstruck when: she walked past Aerosmith singer Steven Tyler
pet peeve: water bottle sweat! 'You know when the water bottle gets condensation and it just starts getting all wet on the outside! Ew!' says Demi

favourite ice cream flavour: 'Cake Batter Ice Cream from Cold Stone Creamery. With sprinkles on top, OMG, it's so good!'
food glorious food: between *Camp Rock* takes, Demi sipped vanilla tea and Chai lattes. She and Anna Maria were obsessed with ketchup chips. AM spills: 'Demi's mom ordered 20 bags and sent them to her home in Texas, so Demi could have them after *Camp Rock*. They're so good!'

the coolest part of being a teen idol: Demi says the coolest part is travelling the world and sharing it with her family
demi's favourite artists to sing in the shower: The National Anthem, Kelly Clarkson or Paramore

Introducing Demi Lovato

2008 will be remembered as the year that Demetria Devonne "Demi" Lovato won our hearts. The sassy sixteen-year-old singer lit up the screen as Mitchie Torres in Disney Channel's awesome movie, *Camp Rock*, and her debut album *Don't Forget* was a global hit. Surely nothing can stop this girl!

She can act, she's got a great singing voice and plays a number of instruments. The bubbly brunette has killer style, and in *Camp Rock* Joe Jonas was her love interest – that's got to be every girl's dream! With the support of her best-female-friend, Selena Gomez, Demi is set to rock your world. Are you ready?

i keep expecting one day i'm going to wake up and she's going to be different, but she's not. she's the same kid she's always been.'

mom, dianna delagarza

fact: Demi has studied piano, voice, guitar, songwriting, and hip-hop dancing.

early days

While it might seem like Demi's got it all, the star had a difficult childhood. Like so many, Demi comes from a family where the parents are divorced, and trying to divide her time between her mom, stepdad and real dad is quite a task!

Demi was born in Dallas, Texas, to Patrick and Dianna Lovato. Her mom Dianna was a Dallas Cowboys cheerleader and country recording artist; her father, Patrick, moved to New Mexico after his and Dianna's marriage ended. Dianna remarried Eddie, who has raised Demi since she was just one. Eddie is Demi's co-manager and the guy that Demi called 'Dad' as she was growing up. He's always been there for Demi. 'I need him in the mornings and at night and for support,' she says. Eddie was there when Demi realised she wanted to be a singer. Demi got stage fright at her kindergarten talent show, but Eddie cheered her on and she eventually nailed Celine Dion's 'My Heart Will Go On'.

fact: As a kid, Demi loved being on the go and hated to sit still.

fact: Demi has been performing since she was five years old!

Patrick had been fighting cancer for many years and rarely saw Demi. But she shocked him with a surprise visit in February 2008! Reconnecting with his daughter gave Patrick new hope in his fight against cancer.

Ever since Patrick reappeared in her life, Demi must have felt torn between her two dads. Like many teens, Demi is trying to figure out how to make room in her life for her real dad, who she hadn't seen for years, and her stepdad. It goes to show how Demi's homelife is just as complicated as the homelife of so many kids!

fact: During the summer, Demi likes to swim in her backyard. 'We have a really cool pool back home – it's like saltwater and dark blue and really crazy.'

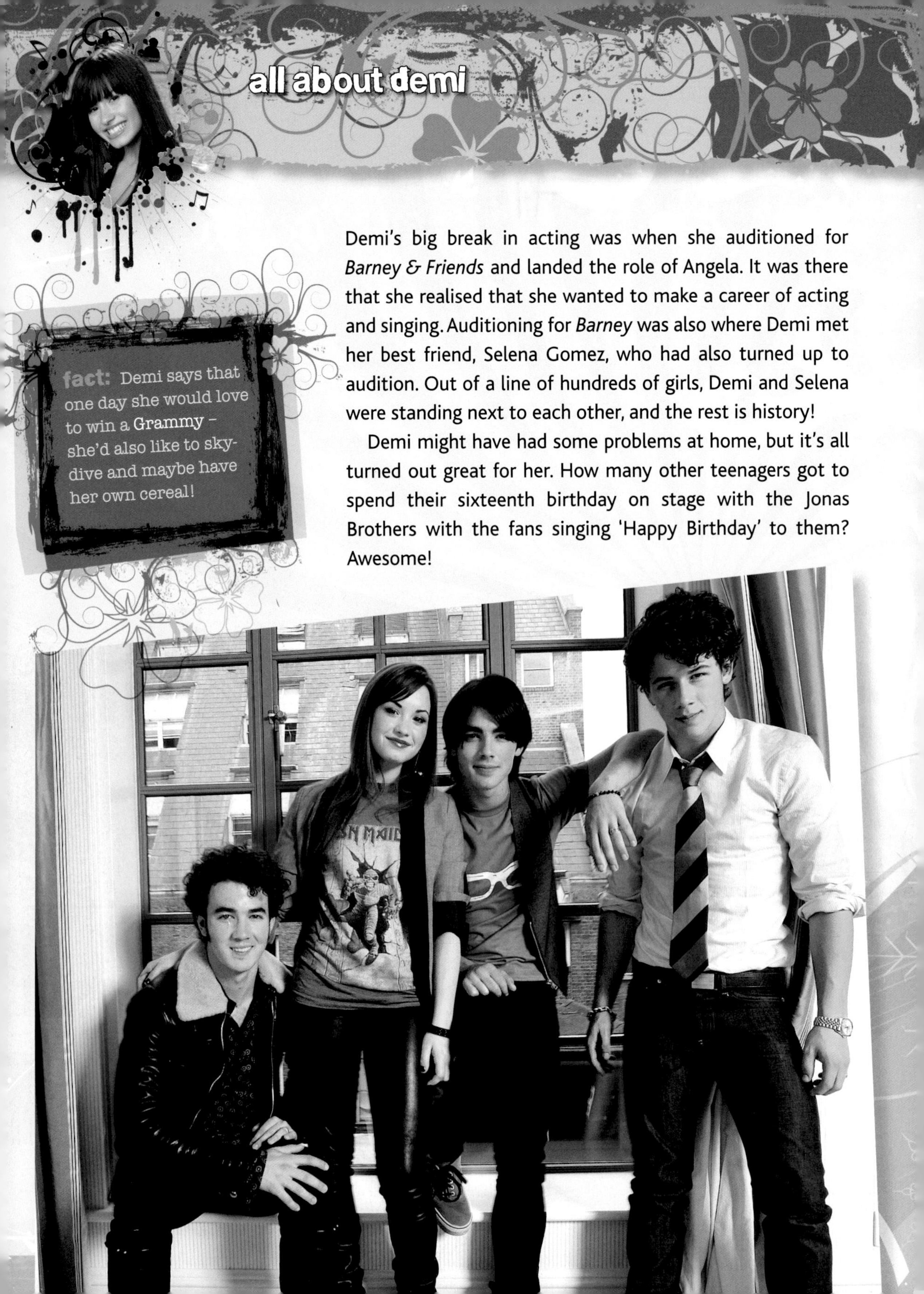

all about demi

Demi's big break in acting was when she auditioned for *Barney & Friends* and landed the role of Angela. It was there that she realised that she wanted to make a career of acting and singing. Auditioning for *Barney* was also where Demi met her best friend, Selena Gomez, who had also turned up to audition. Out of a line of hundreds of girls, Demi and Selena were standing next to each other, and the rest is history!

Demi might have had some problems at home, but it's all turned out great for her. How many other teenagers got to spend their sixteenth birthday on stage with the Jonas Brothers with the fans singing 'Happy Birthday' to them? Awesome!

fact: Demi says that one day she would love to win a **Grammy** – she'd also like to sky-dive and maybe have her own cereal!

horoscope: leo

Demi is a classic Leo gal. She loves to dream big and also gets everyone's attention. Her friends are also very important to her. Calm and peace-loving, Demi's friends find her to be soothing – she really chills them out. Although she's gentle, she can also be pretty stubborn and doesn't like change! When it comes to crushing, Demi is looking for a guy who is charming, funny and full of life, just like she is! Leos are supercreative, just like Demi.

Chapter 2 School Rules!

school life

School was fun for Demi but she wishes she had focused more on her schoolwork rather than being popular. 'I think Mitchie should have done that too – just focused more on having a good time at camp rather than being popular. It ends badly if you're trying to impress someone,' says Demi. Although she's home-schooled now, it's a little known fact that while Demi was at school she was bullied.

demi: 'i wasn't shy at school. **i was very outgoing**. i was pretty much the same person as i am now, but **i didn't know who i was**. i got caught up in what people were doing. i was kind of socially awkward. i had **more fun** as i started home-schooling.'

Although it might seem like Demi is the girl who's got it all, even she suffered at the hands of mean girls at school. Bullying can happen to anyone, but as Demi shows, it's important to stay positive and not let those mean girls win!

fact: At school, girls called Demi fat and ugly. 'They called me everything! Learning to ignore it is the toughest thing I've ever gone through.'

bullying

'I think getting backstabbed by a friend is just part of growing up,' says Demi. 'There were girls I dealt with at my school I thought were my best friends, who just turned on me, and that made it really hard.' These girls would spread rumours about Demi, and call her names.

'They were just being bullies,' says Demi. 'I would call my mum crying and say "Please take me out of school!" It's better to tell someone. Sometimes they can't do anything because it's verbal abuse, but don't let it affect you. Girls will be more vicious and mean than boys. You can't listen to them and give them what they want. I continued to be nice to them. I didn't give in to what they wanted or fight them. You have to be like, "If that's how you feel, great. I'm going to do what I love."'

This bunch of mean girls must have made Demi feel terrible and insecure. Demi was in the seventh grade, and she didn't do anything on Friday or Saturday nights. 'In fact, I had to be home-schooled because I was threatened by bullies so much,' she says. But being home-schooled was the best decision Demi ever made, because that's when she picked up her guitar, because she was so lonely. 'It was like my therapy!' she says. 'I just had a lot of fun and focused on music and acting more.'

Even though the mean girls made her feel bad, it didn't stop Demi being a good student. 'I was a good student!' she says. 'When I started home-schooling, I tested two grades above where I should be. But I could have done so much more.' Demi wishes that when she was at school she had cared less about being popular and focused more on her schoolwork.

get demi's locker look!

Q. how was your locker decorated?

demi: 'It had a mirror so I could check my make-up – every girl had one! I had pictures of my friends and me. By sixth grade, it was totally decorated, but I got so sick of having to reorganise it all the time, so in seventh grade, it was just a stack of books!'

Q. how would you decorate your locker today?

demi: 'I'd paint the front black, so I'd have the only black locker in the school. I'd spray paint "Demi" in neon, which would totally not be acceptable in school, but it would be nice to imagine! I'd hang pictures of The Jonas Brothers, Jim Sturgess, William Beckett, and Nikki Sixx in his good days. I love, love him!'

demi: 'i was always **a tomboy** and hung out with the guys in fifth grade, so when i went to junior high for the first day, i **wore a little dress** or a skirt. i wore make-up and did my hair and everyone looked at me, like **"who's that?"** it was cool!'

school fashion

Demi's well known for her snappy dress sense and she's always loved fashion, even through school! Her favourite first-day-of-school outfit was for the start of sixth grade. 'I can't remember if it was a skirt or a dress,' she says. 'I usually wore something very cute. Maybe it was a sundress. It was never rock – which is so weird. Since I started home-schooling, I got more in touch with who I am and I realized rock is the way to go. So now, I'd wear neon leggings with a leather jacket.'

today

Recently Demi met up with the same mean girls who were nasty to her at in school. Demi says, 'They were all like, "It's so good to see you!" And I was like, "Really? Remember when you wrote on the bathroom walls how much you hated me, and I had to leave school?" Those girls threatened me. One day the popular girls wrote a hate letter, a petition, which said "If anyone hates Demi, sign this letter" and it got passed around school. Everyone who wanted to be popular signed it. They'd stand across my yard yelling. It was really bad, so I started home-schooling. My best friend Selena home-schooled with me to make sure I was ok. It was the true act of a best friend, and she was the only friend I had for about a year and a half!'

Selena was there to make sure Demi didn't feel put down, because she's worth more than that! Demi will never forget the experience she had with the mean girls, but with buddies like Selena, she's gained the confidence to move on. True friends are the best things ever!

Chapter 3

CAMP ROCK!!!

early work

She might be Disney's hottest property right now, but many years back Demi had to go along and audition, just like all the other kids. She went along to audition for *Barney & Friends* when she was just five years old, but she was turned away because she didn't know how to read yet. The following year, after she had learned to read, Demi went along to audition again, and met her best friend Selena Gomez while waiting in line. Both girls got parts in *Barney & Friends* and spent two seasons on the show together.

After her time with the cuddly purple dinosaur, Demi had some guest roles on programmes like *Prison Break*, *Split Ends* and *Just Jordan*. She just couldn't get that big break. But finally it came at a Disney talent search in her hometown of Dallas. Demi won a role on *As the Bell Rings*, which was a short series that ran between the longer shows on the Disney Channel.

Demi was super excited! 'Even though the show was only, like, five minutes long, it was the Disney Channel!' she says. 'I thought it was the coolest thing.'

But Demi was also scared. 'When I got the part, I actually cried. I thought, I'm not going to be able to do this – I'm not funny! I'm never going to be able to work for the Disney Channel, because they're based on comedy.' How wrong she was! Not only is Demi a super-talented actress, dancer and

demi's camp rock embarrassing moment

'I was swinging on a swing and one of the cameras off set was shooting behind the scenes stuff for *Camp Rock*. I fell off from the underneath and it hit me on the head. The cameraman got that on video, so that was pretty embarrassing!'

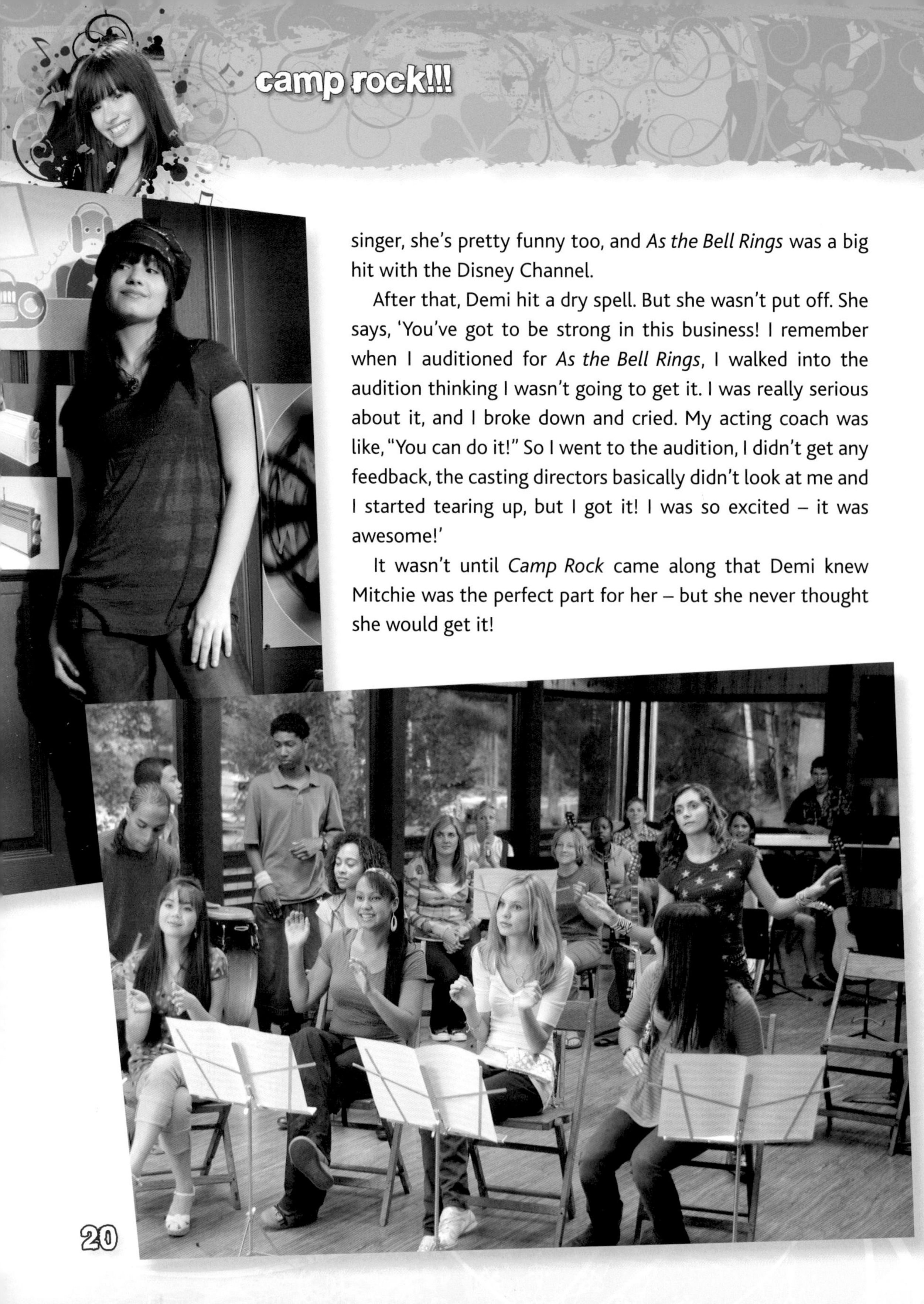

singer, she's pretty funny too, and *As the Bell Rings* was a big hit with the Disney Channel.

After that, Demi hit a dry spell. But she wasn't put off. She says, 'You've got to be strong in this business! I remember when I auditioned for *As the Bell Rings*, I walked into the audition thinking I wasn't going to get it. I was really serious about it, and I broke down and cried. My acting coach was like, "You can do it!" So I went to the audition, I didn't get any feedback, the casting directors basically didn't look at me and I started tearing up, but I got it! I was so excited – it was awesome!'

It wasn't until *Camp Rock* came along that Demi knew Mitchie was the perfect part for her – but she never thought she would get it!

camp rock

The Disney film *Camp Rock* was a big hit, and really put the spotlight on Demi!

The story begins in the home of Mitchie Torres (Demi Lovato), a young musician who hopes to become a singer. Mitchie wants to attend Camp Rock but her parents can't afford to send her. Mitchie's mom decides to take her cooking business to Camp Rock, so Mitchie can go if she helps her mom out in the kitchen.

When Mitchie arrives at camp she makes friends with a few people including Caitlyn Gellar (Alyson Stoner) and Lola Scott (Aaryn Doyle). Mitchie meets Camp Rock diva, Tess Tyler (Meaghan Jette Martin), the daughter of pop star T.J. Tyler (Jennifer Ricci), and her so-called 'best friends', Peggy Warburton (Jasmine Richards) and Ella Shang (Anna Maria Perez de Tagle).

Meanwhile, spoiled brat/pop star Shane Gray (Joe Jonas) is sent to camp by his bandmates Jason (Kevin Jonas) and Nate (Nick Jonas). Because of his bad attitude, he has to be in charge of dance classes for one month at Camp Rock. Later that day, Shane is chased by fans and has to hide in the bushes. He hears Mitchie singing, and he swears he will find the girl who was singing, but he just can't find her!

Because Mitchie is so desperate to fit in, she lies to Tess and says that her mother is the president of Hot Tunes TV China. Tess, Peggy, and Ella are impressed, and invite Mitchie to be friends with them. Mitchie has to hide in the kitchen when she is helping her mother so no-one recognises her.

how does demi compare to mitchie torres?
'We're both figuring out who we are. I used to be insecure. I didn't know where I fit in until I found music.'

Joe Jonas - Shane Gray

Kevin Jonas – Jason

Nick Jonas – Nate

Shane and Mitchie see each other again at the lake where he's writing a song. Later that day, Caitlyn is sent to kitchen duty after a food fight with Tess. In the kitchen, Caitlyn finds out that Mitchie is really the cook's daughter! She threatens to tell everyone, but decides not to when Mitchie stands up for her in another fight with Tess. It turns out that Caitlyn used to be best friends with Tess.

Shane begins to search for the mystery girl with the beautiful voice, but he can't find her. Tess finds out about Mitchie and Shane's friendship and also finds out about Mitchie's secret. She tells everyone the secret, which breaks Shane's heart, as he thinks that Mitchie was only friends with him because he's famous. Everyone turns against Mitchie because they realise that she lied to them.

Tess hides her precious charm bracelet between some of Mitchie's books in the kitchen to make it look like Mitchie stole it. Her scheme works, and Caitlyn and Mitchie are banned from all camp activities until the end of Final Jam.

Right before Final Jam, Tess falls out with Peggy and Ella. Tess enters Final Jam but sees her mother talking on her phone instead of listening to her performance. Upset, Tess drops out of the competition by nearly falling off the stage to get her mom's attention and runs off the stage crying.

A last minute addition is performed by Peggy. After Peggy sings, Tess apologises to her and Ella, saying she never realised that

Alyson Stoner - Caitlyn Gellar

Aaryn Doyle – Lola Scott

Meaghan Jette Martin - Tess Tyler

Peggy was so good. As Shane, Nate, and Jason are judging, Mitchie performs her song. Shane realises that Mitchie is the girl with the voice he was searching for, and he sings along with her. Peggy wins Final Jam, Tess apologises to Mitchie and Caitlyn, and admits that her bracelet wasn't stolen after all. Finally, the whole camp sings one song together: We Rock!!!

Jasmine Richards - **Peggy Dupree**

demi lovato versus mitchie torres!

Demi sang Aretha Franklin's 'Ain't No Way' for her *Camp Rock* audition, and it blew the casting agents away. Although Demi should have been totally stoked to have got the role of Mitchie, she was still nervous. 'I never wanted a part more than this in my life!' she says. And who could blame her – Mitchie was the role of a lifetime!

But *Camp Rock* was more than just a great film to be in. It was also a turning point in Demi's life for her personally. '*Camp Rock* was when I really broke out of my shell,' says Demi. 'My character, Mitchie, is like me. We were both pretty shy when it came to rocking out on stage and always wanted to fit in, until we learned to stand out in a crowd! Now that my dreams have come true, it's made me want to set even bigger goals!'

Meaghan Martin and Jasmine Richards play the mean girls in *Camp Rock*, but in real life, the girls are all tight! 'We are all so close I cried when it was time to go,' says Demi. Another part of the film that was different in real life was the canoe scene with Joe Jonas. 'There were 40 camera people connected to the canoe!' laughs Demi. 'It was awkward because they were saying, "Look into each other's eyes," and that's hard to do without laughing!'

Anna Maria Perez de Tagle - **Ella Shang**

demi: 'mitchie is pretty shy. she was insecure at first, but she realises who she is at the camp and comes into her own. i can relate to her because i was the same way before the movie. when i was filming in canada, i really found out who i was. i was insecure before i came as i was doing the scene where i rock out on stage at the end, i evolved.'

camp rock co-stars

tess tyler

aka - meaghan martin

full name: Meaghan Jette Martin

birthday: February 17, 1992

born in: Las Vegas, Arizona, USA

favourite colour: pink

favourite sport: competitive shopping!

best places to shop: Urban Outfitters, Planet Funk, J Crew, Betsey Johnson, and Nordstrom

camp rock fact: she used *Mean Girls*'s actress Regina George as her inspiration for her role as Tess in *Camp Rock*

'My character is evil to Demi Lovato's character, Mitchie, in *Camp Rock*. But in real life, Demi and I are like best friends! I spent last New Year's Eve in Texas with Demi for five days. We also text each other all the time! We send texts like "You're beautiful" and "I just love you!" constantly.'

caitlyn gellar

aka - alyson stoner

full name: Alyson Rae Stoner

birthday: August 11, 1993

born in: Toledo, Ohio, USA

fact: Alyson sucked her thumb until she was 6

fact: Alyson has been a dancer for Missy Elliot and Eminem

favourite sport: basketball

'*Camp Rock* is all about standing up for yourself and finding your own style and being an individual and embracing your voice. It's knowing that no matter what strengths other people have, you also have your individual strengths that you were born with – and you should play those up and not worry about what everyone else is saying. I think that every person can relate to that in their own way.'

margaret 'peggy' dupree

aka - jasmine richards

full name: Jasmine Richards
birthday: June 28, 1990
born in: Scarborough, Ontario, Canada
favourite actresses: Halle Barry and Meryl Streep
fact: Jasmine loves to change her hairstyle all the time
her opinion on boys:
'You love em' and you hate em.'

'I think my character is such a good role model for kids because it just proves that someone can do anything even if they're being held back by that one person who's slightly above them – like the mean girl or the popular girl from school. You can always just stand up and be yourself.'

ella shang

aka - anna maria perez de taglé

full name: Anna Maria Francesca Enriquez Perez de Taglé
birthday: December 23, 1990
born in: San Francisco, California, USA
favourite colour: red
favourite drinks: Gatorade, water
She can swim and ski
anna maria's camp rock funny moment: A scene where Joe [Jonas] was supposed to yell at Demi but kept laughing instead!

'I think kids will be able to relate to this movie just because it has good morals. It says to never be somebody you're not and always be yourself and ... also to break out of your shell. If you've got a talent and you know you have a talent, you've got to be confident and show everyone.'

'My character is a girly-girl and she's obsessed with lip gloss and her hair, shoes, and clothes. I'm a fashionista too.'

the jobros

demi: 'it was a dream to work with joe jonas. any fifteen-year-old girl would say so!'

Demi totally loved working with the Jonas Brothers, and says that they are complete gentlemen and are the coolest guys she'll ever meet. 'Every person in *Camp Rock* was staying at the same hotel,' says Demi. 'The Jonas brothers would always hold a party in their room. They were like, "Hey Demi, dance party, my room, five minutes!" It was fun.'

The cast of *Camp Rock* totally hung out off-set too. Last Halloween Demi and the *Camp Rock* girls had the cutest Halloween dates in town – the Jonas Brothers! Demi says 'I was in LA with the cast of *Camp Rock* and we all dressed up as the cast of *High School Musical*! It was so much fun! I was Gabriella, and Joe went as Troy. Anna Maria dressed up as Ryan, and she had a blonde wig on – it was funny!' After the cast got loads of yummy goodies, JoBros threw a sweet after-party, and all the cast members went and played hide and seek in the boys' backyard. Nick was definitely the best at hiding – no-one could find him because he was up trees and on the roof!

demi: 'in rehearsals, joe was dancing on stage and he didn't notice where he was going. he completely dances off the stage and just falls. it's one of those moments that, every time i think about it, i just laugh.'

jobros facts!!!

joe jonas

full name: Joseph Adam Jonas
birthday: August 15th, 1989
born in: Casa Grande, Arizona, USA
favourite colour: blue
hobbies: making movies, jogging and working out
favourite movie: *High School Musical* movies, also *School for Scoundrels* and *Dumb & Dumber*
most ridiculous new year's resolution: to talk to animals
fact: Joe loves working out, running, swimming, and playing soccer
fact: One day Joe would like to visit the moon!
joe's camp rock moment: when Joe was filming *Camp Rock*, he said his most embarrassing moment was when he was punched in the stomach and farted!

joe on demi: 'Demi is fun, very mature, and always there when you need a friend.'

joe on demi:

'Demi Lovato's voice is amazing!'

'*Camp Rock* has a really amazing message that all the kids can relate to ... You realise how you're always trying to fit into the cool crowd, and everyone goes through that and the peer pressure from that. I know I did while I was growing up – even at camp, I definitely wanted to hang out with the cool kids, and I was trying to be something I'm not. I think this movie really shows that you can be who you are and you can hang out with the friends that you're comfortable with.'

nick jonas

full name: Nicholas Jerry Jonas
birthday: September 16th, 1992
born in: Dallas, Texas
favourite colour: blue
hobbies: music, songwriting, baseball, collecting baseball cards, tennis
favourite movie: *Finding Neverland*
hidden talents: playing the drums, breakdancing, one-handed cartwheels.
health fact: Nick's eyes are supersensitive to light
sleep fact: Nick can fall asleep in the most uncomfortable positions
most ticklish spot: feet

'Personally, I find the acting thing to be a little more difficult than music. It's fun, but I sometimes get nervous around the cameras – I forget my lines and stuff like that.'

kevin jonas

full name: Paul Kevin Jonas II
birthday: November 5th, 1987
born in: Teaneck, New Jersey, USA
favourite colour: green
hobbies: playing guitar, bowling
favourite movie: *High School Musical* movies and *About a Boy*
hidden talents: Kevin is good at skateboarding and ping-pong
fact: Kevin shares a bedroom with younger brother Joe
fact: Kevin always loved being the oldest because he bossed his brothers around
fact: Kevin's favorite songs from the *Camp Rock* soundtrack are 'We Rock' and 'Too Cool'.

'While we were filming *Camp Rock* I felt like the older brother to the whole cast.'

'Jason is a little out there, a little spacey, but I love it. I get to be a little loopy, and it's kind of fun.'

the message of camp rock

demi: 'The theme of the movie is to be yourself and not worry about being popular. That's what I had to worry about in middle school. I was always worried about being popular. Wow, if I had a chance to do it over again, I'd so rather be a nerd than be popular – it's so much less stressful and you can be yourself!'

Chapter 4

MuSic

music and touring

Demi's been a busy girl. Not only has she starred in one of the hottest movies ever, she also found time to release a best-selling album and go on tour with the Jonas Brothers! She opened up for JoBros on their *Burning Up* tour, and had a total blast.

fact: DEMI'S GOOD LUCK RITUAL
Before every performance, Demi prays with her band, and does a handshake. Demi also calls her mom for good luck.

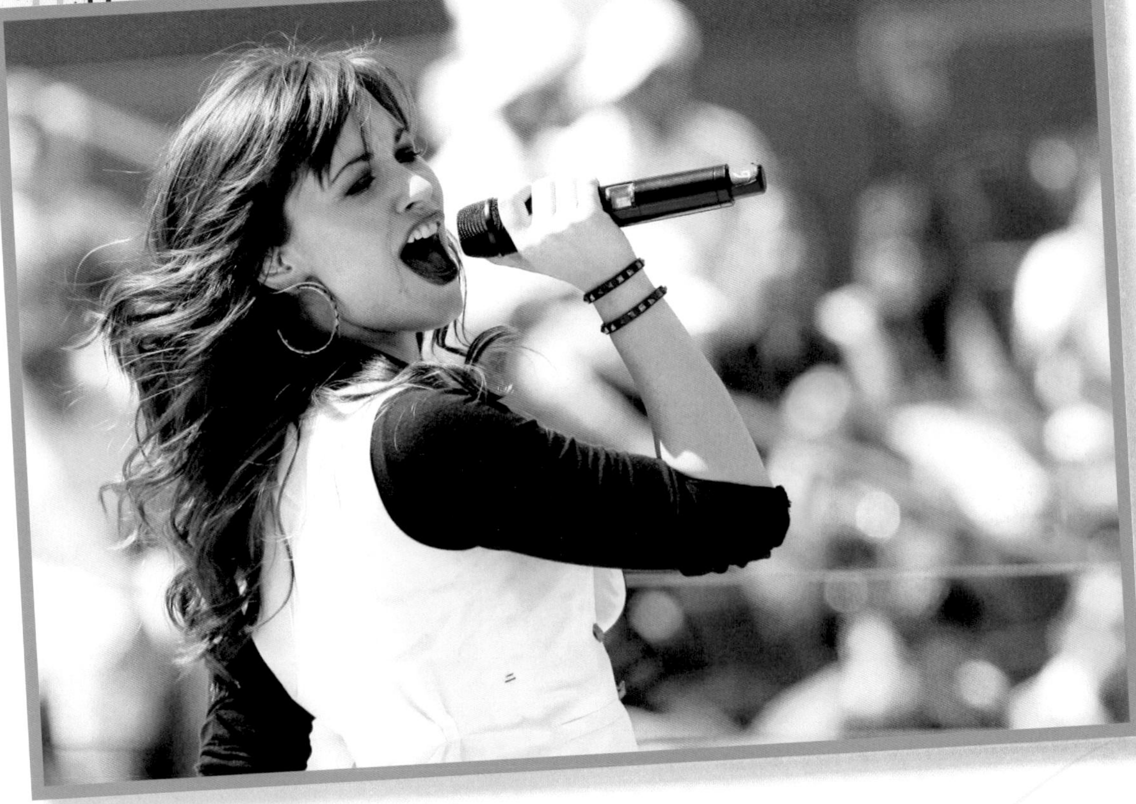

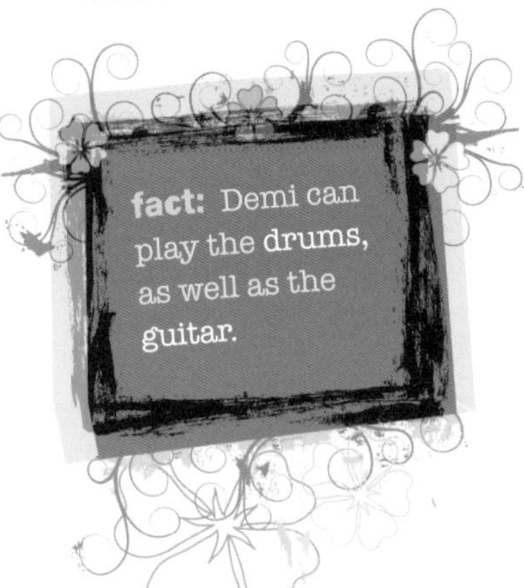

Some of the songs that Demi wrote – 'Stronger', 'Open' and 'Shadow' – were also featured on *As the Bell Rings*, so it made sense for her to release a full album! *Don't Forget* was released in September and was a huge smash worldwide.

When Demi started putting together songs for her album, she realised she might need some outside help. 'I'm more of a writer whose stuff wouldn't make it on a Disney album,' she says. 'It's too dark. My mom's like "Gosh, go to therapy", so I went to The Jonas Brothers saying, "Umm, I need help writing catchy stuff because my audience isn't into metal music!"' So the Jonas Brothers helped her with writing some songs on her album.

demi's backstage must-have:
'I have to have potato chips. The grease and the oil help your throat.' Demi's also a gadget freak – she loves her phone and her laptop, so she always takes lots of gadgets on the road!

demi can't live without her guitar!
'I can't stop singing, I can't stop writing, I can't stop playing!'

demi's message to her fans:
'you guys seriously rock. I love you and thanks for the support!'

on being on tour with jonas brothers:
'They don't really have any nasty habits. They probably take longer to get ready than I do!'

demi's dream duet:
'Kelly Clarkson, Paramore, or The Academy – they're cute!'

on songwriting:
'Every song I write now I can relate to because I'm growing. I'm going through more stuff than when I was 10! I've been really using it as therapy.'

And don't expect it to be too much like *Camp Rock* – Demi's album is different from what you've heard before! '*Camp Rock* is more Disney-related. My stuff is definitely rock. It has a Southern rock feel to it. It's different. It's like nothing you've heard on Disney. Nick was doing the chords and I was doing the lyrics,' says Demi. 'Then we'd collaborate and change things!'

Demi loves all the songs on her album, but she says the song she connected with the most was 'Don't Forget'. 'It's very personal,' she says. 'When you hear the song, it's self-explanatory. It's about a heartbreak.' She says that she thinks her fans will enjoy the song 'Get Back' the most. 'You don't want to listen to sad songs all the time!' says the bubbly brunette, 'and this song's just very fun, and it's about wanting to get back with somebody. It's like telling a guy, "I know that you miss me". It's really upbeat. It's awesome.'

Lots of people have been comparing Demi to a certain other Disney favourite – Miley Cyrus! But Demi doesn't see it. 'I don't see myself as the next Miley – I just see myself as Demi – Miley is amazing and has built a hugely successful career, so I respect that. It's just that, again, we're two totally different artists – and there's room for everyone to be themselves in this business. I'm just trying to be Demi right now!' Good for her!

Chapter 5

Demi's Hot Style

Demi's style is totally unmissable. This hot talent has great taste in clothes!

Her main influence is the '80s, although there's no one person she says she looks to for style tips. 'I don't really have a personal style icon. But I like reading fashion magazines, they have a bunch of crazy outfits and stuff, so I get influenced by that, and mannequins in stores inspire me a lot!'

demi's hot style

demi: 'i love to wear vintage concert t-shirts. i have a rock vibe on stage.'

demi fashion fact: She has a necklace that says 'True Love Waits'.

This bubbly brunette rocks a mixture of styles, and she's so confident she can pull them all off! She loves accessorizing, and that means hats, cool belts and awesome bags. She's not just a glamorous tomboy either – at premieres, you can catch Demi looking feminine in LBDs (little black dresses) and heels!

Although she suffered bullying in the past, Demi is strong and refuses to feel bad about herself. 'Everyone gets a little self-conscious when they look in the mirror,' she says, 'but I don't ever pinpoint anything I don't like about myself.' Demi's a great role model for other girls too. She says her best feature is her waist. 'I'm not the type of toothpick skinny girl, you know,' she says. 'I've got curves and I accentuate them with belts!'

demi's insecurity: At a recent photo shoot Demi and her mom Dianne revealed that growing up, Demi was teased about her chin cleft and she became self-conscious about it.

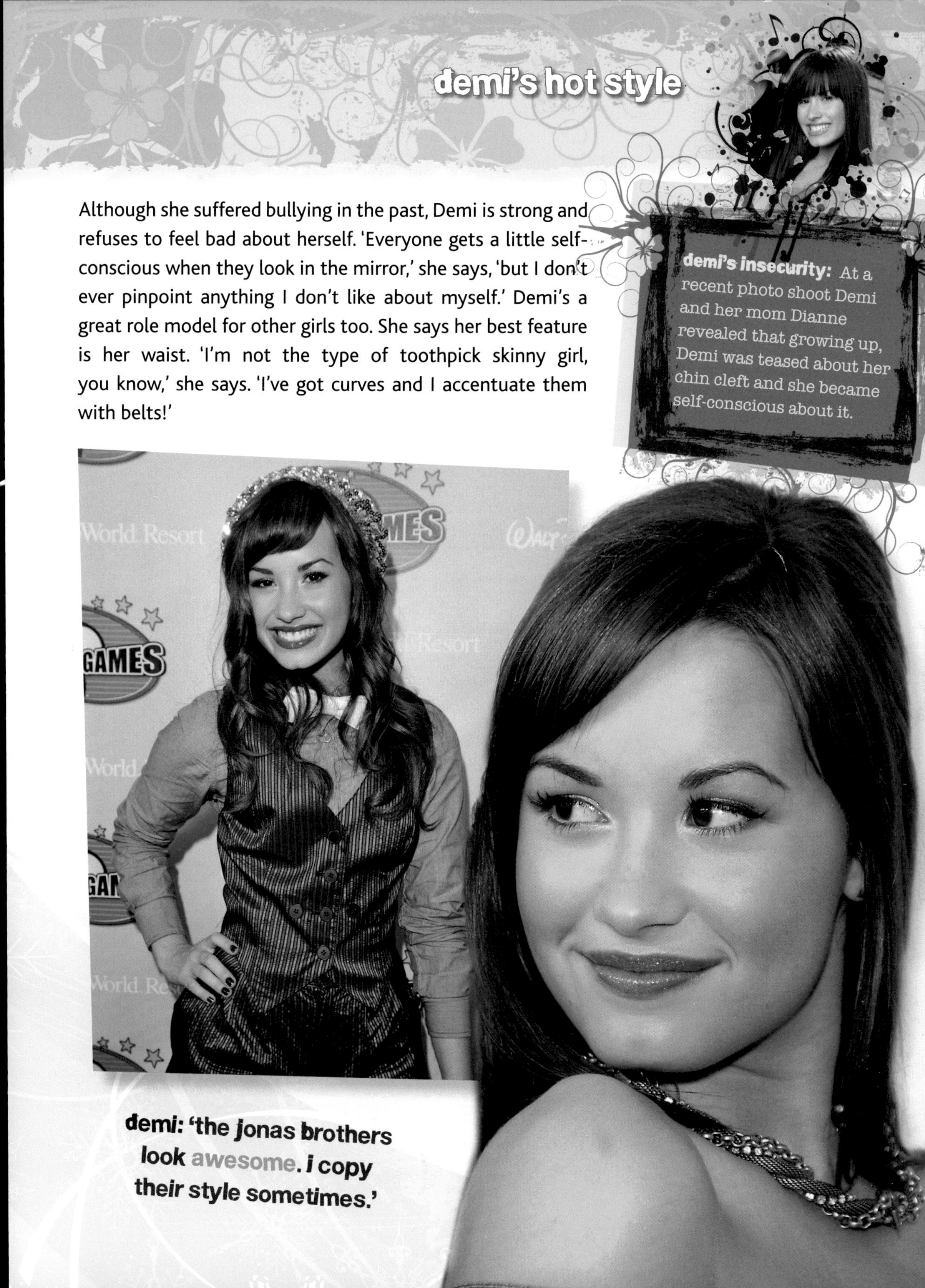

demi: 'the jonas brothers look awesome. i copy their style sometimes.'

stores demi loves: Forever 21 for clothes, Aldo for shoes.

Demi has a great wardrobe, but her stepdad and co-manager Eddie keeps a close eye on the teen to make sure she doesn't do anything too crazy. During a photo shoot, Demi pleaded with her stepdad Eddie to let her dye her hair black for the *Burning Up* tour. He said no! But he did compromise when Demi asked about going a darker brown.

Demi's advice on accepting the way you look: 'The best advice I've ever gotten is not to let people get to you. You can't change everyone's opinion about you because there's always going to be a hater. You just have to take it with a pinch of salt and move on!' Right on, sister!

demi style must-have: her hair tools.

Chapter Six

Best Friends Forever!

It's no secret that Demi has one very special friend in her world: fellow Disney actress Selena Gomez.

BFFs since age seven, Selena and Demi met at a *Barney* audition. 'We were in line with 1400 other kids, and we happened to be standing next to each other.' As the girls were both from Texas, they instantly hit it off. Demi used to have BBQs at her house every weekend. Her dad's longtime friends would come over, and Selena and Demi would swim. 'Even when I was 8 – that was when I first got the pool – me and Selena would play acting out scenes in the pool,' says Demi. The entire time,

all about selena!

full name: Selena Marie Gomez
birthday: July 22, 1992
born in: New York City, USA
pets: she has four dogs, one of them she named Chip
heritage: Selena is of Mexican and Italian descent
favourite shoes: Converse (she owns over 20 pairs!)
favourite pizza toppings: cheese, mushrooms, and jalapenos
most ticklish spot: her feet

xxx

selena: 'i'm not **confident** in myself, so i get down on myself and i believe some of the online stuff. demi's the kind of person who **is honest with me**, and there to **support me** and tell me **"don't listen to that. know who you are."** and that really means a lot to me - because **she's honest** with me and really harsh, but she does it because **she loves me**.'

I remember us playing mermaids, and I was the mermaid who was a diva or whatever. We were totally acting out the whole time – it was so great!'

To this day, the girls share everything – absolutely everything! Demi says, 'It's pretty mutual. Selena will go through my makeup bag and be like, "Hey, isn't this my eyeliner and eye shadow brush?" and I'll be like "Yeah, about that, sorry!" and she'll be like "No, it's cool". Then I'll go to her hotel room and say "Hey, aren't those my shoes?" and she's like, "Yeah!"'

The girls have also shared the same acting coach (Cathy Linley, Cody Linley's mum) and share each other's clothes at red carpet events. 'At the first premiere I went to with her, Selena was wearing all my clothes! We always borrow each other's jeans, and we have Converse and switch them by accident,' Demi spills!

As the girls are both actresses, you might think they would fight over parts. Not so. These two buddies are so close that they just want the best for each other. 'We've talked about being competitive,' says Demi. 'We've known since we were young that we have the same image. We're both Hispanic and have dark hair – it's just one of those things. We would drive three hours to an audition in Austin, and my mom would say if one of us gets something, it's better than none of us getting something. So whoever gets it, we're happy for each other.'

As a sign of their friendship, today Selena and Demi wear matching guitar pick necklaces, and have nicknames for each other: Selena calls Demi 'Dem', and Demi calls Selena 'Dork'! Having suffered at the hands of mean bullies at school, Demi knows how important true friends are. That's why she and Selena are so tight! 'I'm one of the luckiest girls ever,' says Demi. 'I couldn't ask for a better friend. She's one of the greatest people. She's sweet, hilarious, intelligent and down

to earth. If there's one thing that separates her from other people I know it's that she's genuine. She was my rock! I'm thankful to say I've had her throughout my life.'

These two BFFs have had some crazy times too. Their best adventure, according to Selena, was going through the rainforest together! 'Demi looked so glamorous, it was hilarious,' says Selena. 'I had on shorts and Converse. She had on zebra leggings, so she would match the rainforest, and Ray Bans. That was our most fun and crazy adventure because we didn't know what to expect.'

demi: 'selena and i were at the movies and spotted chris brown. i was like, "i want to ask him for his autograph." selena wouldn't, but i did! she even snapped a photo with chris!'

So does Demi miss Selena when she's not around? 'Sometimes if I haven't seen her since yesterday afternoon, I'm like, "Where is Selena?" So I'll be texting her – like right now! It's not just because of how long we've known each other – since we were seven years old – she was there for me. There are some friends you don't know if they're only friends with you because you're making it.'

demi: 'i think the toughest thing for me is being able to tell myself that i'm beautiful. selena totally helped me with growing up and dealing with a changing figure and face. she's always been there for me.'

demi loves sleepovers

'Selena and I take every chance we get to have sleepovers!' The girls like staying up late to chat about JoBros and make YouTube vids. Demi's favourite sleepover was when she and Selena dressed up really crazy and went to a department store. 'We walked around to see if people would stare at us and think we were crazy. And they totally did!' OMG – so much fun! But Demi and Selena like staying in too. 'I remember playing Barbies with Selena when at a sleepover in fourth grade. We were dressing the dolls up, and we stayed up till five in the morning playing! We acted out movies with the Barbies!'

sleepover essentials!

Want to have an awesome sleepover, in Demi and Selena style? Here's what you'll need ...

scary movies! They like watching cheesy scary movies, like *I Know What You Did Last Summer*!

popcorn! The girls love junk food when they're having sleepovers, especially popcorn

pickles! 'I know it sounds weird but me and Selena always eat pickles whenever we hang out. They're so good!' says Demi!

perfect playlist! The girls need to have the best tunes when they're hanging out – Paramore's album *Riot* is their favourite!

princess protection program

demi: **'i've said it many times, but each time** i mean it more and more **- she is a true friend. i can trust her and that's not something you come across** in this town **or this business!'**

The girls' close friendship even inspired Disney to make a series about them! *Princess Protection Program* stars friends Selena and Demi together in it. When Princess Rosalina (Demi) is threatened by an evil dictator, she is whisked away and placed into the Princess Protection Program, a secret agency that watches over imperiled princesses around the world. Mason, an agent with the program, hides Princess Rosalina in his own home where, with the help of his daughter Carter (Selena), she adopts the cover of an ordinary teen named Rosie. An insecure tomboy, Carter works at a local bait shop after school and dreams of going to the school dance with her crush, Donny, the school hunk. Rosie quickly becomes popular at school but the two also form a close bond as Carter helps Rosie transform into a normal teenager and Rosie shows Carter how to find the princess within herself! 'Disney Channel loved our friendship,' says Selena, 'and they wanted to do something about that. She had *Camp Rock* and I was doing *Wizards*, and we were already working for Disney Channel and they wanted to market that.'

other pals

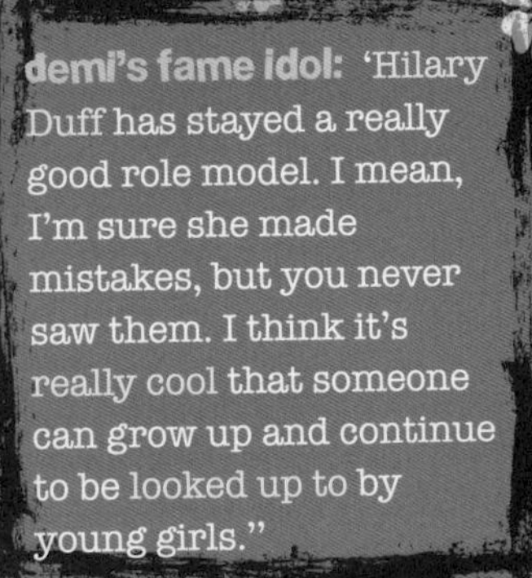

demi's fame idol: 'Hilary Duff has stayed a really good role model. I mean, I'm sure she made mistakes, but you never saw them. I think it's really cool that someone can grow up and continue to be looked up to by young girls."

Demi also counts a list of other celebrities amongst her buddies, including the Jonas Brothers!

'Joe is a big dork. Nicky is witty and sarcastic – sometimes I think he's the funniest. Kevin plays the older-brother role. They're all really great,' Demi gushes. 'Nick is the funniest person I know, everyone thinks he is so serious, but when you get to know him he's not what you expect. I sit there and just start laughing because he's so witty and sarcastic.' Demi says all the Jonas Brothers are just normal teenage brothers. 'They're just teenage guys. They support each other with everything.'

Demi should know – she spent enough time with them! Not only were they all together for the filming of *Camp Rock*, but she also joined the JoBros on their *Burning Up* tour. The brothers are very protective of her, viewing her like their sister! 'I'm very uncoordinated,' says Demi. 'I'm surprised I don't fall on stage more. The Jonas Brothers were always like, "Watch your step." They're ten times more cool when you meet them and hang out with them all the time. They're hilarious!' What a lucky girl!

Demi is also good friends with Meaghan Jette Martin and Alyson Stoner (from *Camp Rock*). Demi and Meaghan actually spent last New Year's Eve together in Texas! She's also remained tight with her *As the Bell Rings* co-stars, Tony Oller, Seth Ginsberg, Carlson Young, Gabriela Rodriguez and Collin Cole.

demi: 'i'd do anything for my friends!'

Rumours: does demi hate miley?

REAL ANSWER: NO!

After Miley and Mandy posted a video poking fun at Demi and Selena, fans assumed war was declared between the best-female-friend posses. But Demi denies it all! Demi and Miley met at the Disney Channel Games just before Demi went onstage to sing with the JoBros. Demi says, 'Miley was really, really nice and she wished me good luck and we talked about the YouTube thing. She said, "You know people are trying to pit us against each other but you're the sweetest girl and you're so talented and I really want you to succeed!" She's very nice and it was nice of her to wish me good luck and give me advice before I went onstage.'

Chapter 7
Love and Rumours

demi and joe???

Demi might have just played the on-screen love interest to the cutest boy on earth, Joe Jonas, but she insists that off-screen the pair are just friends! 'If I was going to date one of the JoBros, don't you think I would have done it by now?' she giggles. 'I feel so lucky because at first I didn't think the JoBros fans were going to like me because there were a lot of rumours about Joe. But I think once we cleared those up now they kinda understand that I'm like the sister! Me and Joe are just friends.' Phew!

demi's secret crush: 'jim sturgess! he was in across the universe and he's in a movie called 21. in 21 he's hiding his accent, because he's from the uk and i love his very british accent!'

Demi also thinks Jake Gyllenhaal is totally cute! 'I was talking about Jake Gyllenhaal in front of a lot of people at a meeting. I have a huge crush on him, even though he's way too old for me. My mom and everyone looked over, and they were like "Oh my god, you're blushing! You're actually blushing!"'

demi: 'i like loyal guys who are honest with you. i hate when a boy leads you on and then leaves you for another girl. my big sis in dallas tells me, "there's no rush to find a bf right now. you have your whole life for boys!"'

demi's best boy advice:
'Never ever, ever, ever fall over a guy. It's all about the chase. Make him want you by sometimes not calling him back. Don't text or call a guy.'

demi and cody

For a while, Demi took acting lessons from Cathy Linley – none other than Cody Linley's mom! Cody and Demi were both from the same town in Texas, and were friends for over seven years, but never really hit it off until they had an acting class together. They didn't realise their feelings for each other until they had to do a kissing scene. That's what started it all, and according to Demi, 'There was chemistry!'

For their first date, Cody took Demi to The Cheesecake Factory. 'He wore a tie. It was adorable!' At the restaurant they munched on pizza and talked about their friends and *Camp Rock*. Afterwards, Cody took Demi to star-gaze in the park. Cody liked Demi because she's so fun, but the celebrity pair had to call off their romance before it got too serious because they were both too focused on their careers! Demi says the couple are still good friends, and who knows what might happen in the future?

totally cringeworthy moments

As well as having her share of celebrity hotties, Demi's had cringey moments with guys too!

Demi Lovato had an awesome relationship with one of her school's football players, who would give Demi little hugs and flirt with her. 'It was really cute, but I don't think he ever looked at me in that way,' she says. But one day Demi's teacher heard her gushing about the guy in class just as her crush happened to walk by. She goes on, 'My teacher brings him into the room and tells him someone was just talking about him. "Someone in this room has a crush on you," my teacher said. And at this point I was so embarrassed. And he was like "Really? Who?" And everybody pointed to me! I was just sinking into my chair. Afterwards I apologized and he said "No, it's all good," and put his arm around me and gave me a hug. We ended up dating two years later!'

demi: 'when i like someone, a lot of things remind me of him – like a song. he's constantly on my mind.'

first date nightmares!

On one first date, Demi Lovato's mom and stepdad never left her alone with her boyfriend, not even for a second! Demi spills, 'I went to the movies with my boyfriend and it was so embarrassing because they both came. My mom, dad and I picked him up and we all went to the movies. We just sat there, and we didn't even talk the whole time.' Demi says he tried to hold her hand, and she got scared, because she was nervous! 'I didn't know if he'd kiss me or anything. He didn't. And I didn't want him to!' Oh dear!

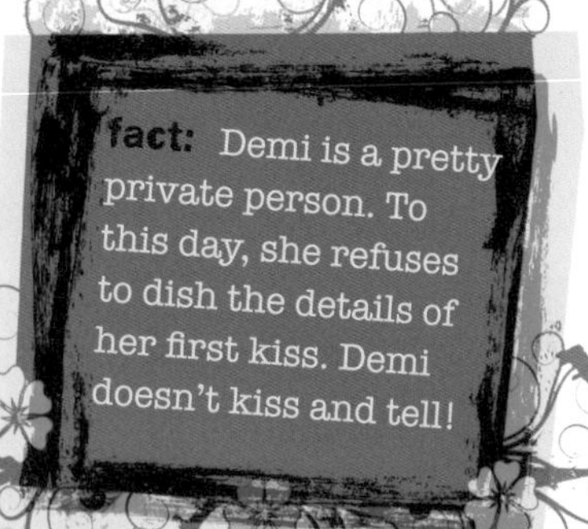

fact: Demi is a pretty private person. To this day, she refuses to dish the details of her first kiss. Demi doesn't kiss and tell!

On another date, Demi was out with a pal on a coffee run, and when she got up to use the bathroom, she spilled her coffee – all over her lap! 'The entire Starbucks cup flipped over and it was completely full! I was wearing a skirt, so the accident made me feel really uncomfortable. I ran to the bathroom and just sat there, like "This is awkward." And I hid my head in my hands, and I was like "Oh my God! This is so embarrassing! I'm sorry, I'm not this clumsy!"'

demi on getting rejected: 'I've been rejected by different crushes several times! The first time I was rejected, I was like, "How do I make him jealous?" But that's not the way to do it. You have to tell yourself, "he's not worth it to me anymore"'

demi today

This bubbly brunette might have had confidence issues in the past, but she's really sure of herself today! 'I don't really care if a boy hears me say I like him,' she says. 'I'm the type of girl who's like: "Oh my gosh, he's so cute. Look at those tight pants!"' Demi also knows she's majorly crushing on someone when she can't stop cracking jokes around them. 'I wouldn't be who I am if I didn't. Part of the reason I'm so corny and into comedy is because all the situations I play have probably happened to me!'

When Demi feels heartache, she turns to the one thing she loves more than anything in the world: to her music. 'To get over a guy, I write about the situation and then I move on! My song 'Trash' is about the first time I got rejected. The guy I was singing about heard the song and said "Wow that's pretty harsh." But I told him, I write what I feel! The song 'Forget' is about really liking someone and having them walk away,' she says.

But who does she think she'll end up with? Does she think it might be an actor or someone famous? 'Guys in the business can be a little bit too confident, you know?' she spills. 'We'll see. I don't know. Hopefully I wanna date, I wanna marry a John Mayer type, really a great musician!'

demi's perfect date:
'I would love to watch the stars on the beach at night.'

demi: 'i like the classic band guy. i once liked a guy who wore black nail polish and a guy who wore black eye makeup. i always go for the more goth-type guys.'

Chapter 8
The Future

After the release of *Camp Rock* nothing was going to stop Demi from becoming an international superstar. She's even been spotted signing autographs and singing outside her hotel in London! And if you're a massive fan of the movie (and come on, who isn't!), you'll be happy to hear that Demi has already signed up to play Mitchie in the sequel. But she won't spill what the new movie is about – 'I'm not even sure what it's going to be about, I swear! I know as much as you do,' she squeals!

princess protection program

As well as *Camp Rock* coming out, going on tour with the Jonas Brothers and releasing her debut album, Demi also spent part of 2008 filming *Princess Protection Program* with BFF, Selena Gomez. PPP is a Disney movie due out in summer 2009, based on the series of the same name. When Princess Rosalina (Demi) is threatened, she is placed into the care of the Princess Protection Program, a secret agency that watches over imperiled princesses around the world. They take her to rural Wisconsin where Mason, an agent with the program, hides Princess Rosalina in his own home. Rosalina adopts the cover of an ordinary teen named Rosie and Mason's daughter, Carter (Selena Gomez), helps Rosie fit in. Rosie quickly becomes popular at school, and she and Carter form a close bond. Carter helps Rosie transform into a normal teenager, while Rosie shows Carter how to find the princess within herself. Demi wrote the theme song for PPP, which is called '2 Worlds Collide'. This song is dedicated to her best friend and co-star, Selena Gomez.

welcome to mollywood / welcome to holliwood / sonny with a chance!

As if that wasn't enough, Demi is also working on a new Disney Channel series, which has already had three titles! First up it was called *Welcome to Mollywood* and Demi was playing lead character Molly. Then it was called *Welcome to Holliwood*, where Demi played lead character Holli!! Now the name has been changed again to confuse everyone. The show is called *Sonny With a Chance*, in which Demi will star as an innocent teen from middle America, called Sonny, who is thrust into the L.A. spotlight when she relocates after landing a role on her favorite show (imagine that!). 'It's very crazy!' says Demi. 'I was nervous in the beginning. It's hard to carry a comedy show. If you're not funny, the show is not going to be funny. I've never had a lot of confidence in comedy, but I've really let loose and totally had fun with it.' Awesome!

demi's life!

But Demi has other ambitions too. She hopes to learn to drive soon! And this screen star also knows there's one thing she'll definitely keep doing: singing and writing music. But she expects her sound to change as she gets older too. 'I want to have a really long music career, so as time goes on I want to get more mature with my music and more soulful,' Demi spills.

For the moment though, Demi has only got one thing on her mind. 'Right now, I just want to rock out and have fun!' she says. And we totally can't wait to see what comes next for Demi!

a message from demi to her fans
'You guys rock.
Thanks so much!
I love you guys!!!!!'
xXx

acknowledgements

Posy Edwards would like to thank Helia Phoenix, Daniel Bunyard, Helen Ewing, Jane Sturrock, Rich Carr, Kate Oliver, Sophie Buchan, Malcolm Edwards and Lisa Milton.

picture credits

Getty: 4 (right), 7, 8 (bottom right), 11, 12, 17 (bottom), 22 (left), 28 (top), 30, 33, 34 (top), 35, 36, 37 (left), 38, 39, 40 (left), 43, 49, 52 (bottom), 53 (left), 55, 57

Rex: 2, 4 (left), 5, 9, 13 (right), 14, 15, 19, 20, 21, 22 (top right & middle right), 24, 25, 26, 28 (bottom), 29, 31, 34 (bottom), 40 (right), 41, 42, 44, 45, 47, 48, 50, 51, 53 (right), 54, 58, 60 (left)

PA Photos: 13 (left), 22 (bottom right), 23, 52 (top right), 63

Mirrorpix: 3, 10, 27, 56,

Corbis: 6, 17 (top), 32, 60 (right)

Big Pictures: 8 (left), 16, 37, 59, 61

First published in hardback in Great Britain in 2009 by Orion Books
an imprint of the Orion Publishing Group Ltd
Orion House, 5 Upper St Martin's Lane, London WC2H 9EA
An Hachette Livre UK Company

1 3 5 7 9 10 8 6 4 2

A CIP catalogue record for this book is available from the British Library.

ISBN: 978 1 4091 1148 1

Designed by www.carrstudio.co.uk
Printed in Spain by Cayfosa

The Orion Publishing Group's policy is to use papers that are natural, renewable and recyclable and made from wood grown in sustainable forests. The logging and manufacturing processes are expected to conform to the environmental regulations of the country of origin.

www.orionbooks.co.uk